2022-2023

Monthly Planner

THIS PLANNER BELONGS TO:

_____

_____

_____

If you have time,
please leave an honest review
on amazon.

It means the world to us!

Personal Information

NAME:		
ADDRESS:		

CITY:	STATE:	ZIP:
PHONE:	MOBILE:	
EMAIL:		

Emergency

NAME:	
RELATIONSHIP:	MOBILE:
EMAIL:	

NAME:	
RELATIONSHIP:	MOBILE:
EMAIL:	

NAME:	
RELATIONSHIP:	MOBILE:
EMAIL:	

NAME:	
RELATIONSHIP:	MOBILE:
EMAIL:	

Contacts

NAME	ADDRESS	PHONE	EMAIL

Contacts

NAME	ADDRESS	PHONE	EMAIL

Contacts

NAME	ADDRESS	PHONE	EMAIL

Contacts

NAME	ADDRESS	PHONE	EMAIL

Passwords

WEBSITE	USERNAME	PASSWORD

Passwords

WEBSITE	USERNAME	PASSWORD

Passwords

WEBSITE	USERNAME	PASSWORD

Passwords

WEBSITE	USERNAME	PASSWORD

Important Dates

DATE	JANUARY

DATE	FEBRUARY

DATE	MARCH

DATE	APRIL

DATE	MAY

DATE	JUNE

Important Dates

DATE	JULY

DATE	AUGUST

DATE	SEPTEMBER

DATE	OCTOBER

DATE	NOVEMBER

DATE	DECEMBER

2022
Year at a Glance

January

Sun	Mon	Tue	Wed	Thu	Fri	Sat
						01
02	03	04	05	06	07	08
09	10	11	12	13	14	15
16	17	18	19	20	21	22
23	24	25	26	27	28	29
30	31					

February

Sun	Mon	Tue	Wed	Thu	Fri	Sat
		01	02	03	04	05
06	07	08	09	10	11	12
13	14	15	16	17	18	19
20	21	22	23	24	25	26
27	28					

March

Sun	Mon	Tue	Wed	Thu	Fri
		01	02	03	04
06	07	08	09	10	11
13	14	15	16	17	18
20	21	22	23	24	25
27	28	29	30	31	

April

Sun	Mon	Tue	Wed	Thu	Fri	Sat
					01	02
03	04	05	06	07	08	09
10	11	12	13	14	15	16
17	18	19	20	21	22	23
24	25	26	27	28	29	30

May

Sun	Mon	Tue	Wed	Thu	Fri	Sat
01	02	03	04	05	06	07
08	09	10	11	12	13	14
15	16	17	18	19	20	21
22	23	24	25	26	27	28
29	30	31				

June

Sun	Mon	Tue	Wed	Thu	Fri
			01	02	03
05	06	07	08	09	10
12	13	14	15	16	17
19	20	21	22	23	24
26	27	28	29	30	

NOTES :

2022
Year at a Glance

July

Mon	Tue	Wed	Thu	Fri	Sat
				01	02
04	05	06	07	08	09
11	12	13	14	15	16
18	19	20	21	22	23
25	26	27	28	29	30

August

Sun	Mon	Tue	Wed	Thu	Fri	Sat
	01	02	03	04	05	06
07	08	09	10	11	12	13
14	15	16	17	18	19	20
21	22	23	24	25	26	27
28	29	30	31			

September

Sun	Mon	Tue	Wed	Thu	Fri	Sat
				01	02	03
04	05	06	07	08	09	10
11	12	13	14	15	16	17
18	19	20	21	22	23	24
25	26	27	28	29	30	

October

Mon	Tue	Wed	Thu	Fri	Sat
					01
03	04	05	06	07	08
10	11	12	13	14	15
17	18	19	20	21	22
24	25	26	27	28	29
31					

November

Sun	Mon	Tue	Wed	Thu	Fri	Sat
		01	02	03	04	05
06	07	08	09	10	11	12
13	14	15	16	17	18	19
20	21	22	23	24	25	26
27	28	29	30			

December

Sun	Mon	Tue	Wed	Thu	Fri	Sat
				01	02	03
04	05	06	07	08	09	10
11	12	13	14	15	16	17
18	19	20	21	22	23	24
25	26	27	28	29	30	31

TES :

2022

	JANUARY	FEBRUARY	MARCH	APRIL	MAY	JUNE
1						
2						
3						
4						
5						
6						
7						
8						
9						
10						
11						
12						
13						
14						
15						
16						
17						
18						
19						
20						
21						
22						
23						
24						
25						
26						
27						
28						
29						
30						
31						

2022

JULY	AUGUST	SEPTEMBER	OCTOBER	NOVEMBER	DECEMBER

January

SUNDAY	MONDAY	TUESDAY	WEDNESDAY
02	03	04	0
09	10	11	
16	17 BIRTHDAY OF MARTIN LUTHER KING, JR.	18	
23 30	24 31	25	2

2022

THURSDAY	FRIDAY	SATURDAY	GOALS
		01 NEW YEAR'S DAY	_____ _____ _____ _____ _____
06	07	08	_____ _____ _____
PHANY			**TO DO LIST**
13	14	15	○ _____ ○ _____ ○ _____ ○ _____
20	21	22	○ _____ ○ _____ ○ _____ ○ _____
27	28	29	○ _____ ○ _____ ○ _____ ○ _____

Notes

Notes

February

SUNDAY	MONDAY	TUESDAY	WEDNESDAY
		01	0
06 SUPER BOWL SUNDAY	07	08	0
13	14 VALENTINE'S DAY	15	
20	21 WASHINGTON'S BIRTHDAY (PRESIDENTS' DAY)	22	2
27	28		

2022

THURSDAY	FRIDAY	SATURDAY
03	04	05
10	11	12
17	18	19
24	25	26

GOALS

_____
_____
_____
_____
_____
_____
_____
_____

TO DO LIST

○ _____
○ _____
○ _____
○ _____
○ _____
○ _____
○ _____
○ _____
○ _____
○ _____
○ _____
○ _____
○ _____
○ _____
○ _____
○ _____
○ _____
○ _____

Notes

Notes

 March

SUNDAY	MONDAY	TUESDAY	WEDNESDAY
		01	0
			ASH WEDNESDAY
06	07	08	0
13	14	15	1
DAYLIGHT SAVING STARTS			
20	21	22	2
27	28	29	3

2022

THURSDAY	FRIDAY	SATURDAY	GOALS
03	04	05	
10	11	12	
17	18	19	
NT PATRICK'S DAY			
24	25	26	
31			

TO DO LIST

- ○ _____
- ○ _____
- ○ _____
- ○ _____
- ○ _____
- ○ _____
- ○ _____
- ○ _____
- ○ _____
- ○ _____
- ○ _____
- ○ _____
- ○ _____
- ○ _____
- ○ _____
- ○ _____
- ○ _____

Notes

Notes

April

SUNDAY	MONDAY	TUESDAY	WEDNESDAY
03	04	05	0
10	11	12	
17 PALM SUNDAY	18	19	
24 EASTER	25	26	

2022

THURSDAY	FRIDAY	SATURDAY	GOALS
	01	02	
	APRIL FOOL'S DAY		
07	08	09	
14	15	16	
MAUNDY THURSDAY	GOOD FRIDAY		
21	22	23	
	EARTH DAY		
28	29	30	

GOALS

_____
_____
_____
_____
_____
_____
_____
_____
_____

TO DO LIST

- ○ _____
- ○ _____
- ○ _____
- ○ _____
- ○ _____
- ○ _____
- ○ _____
- ○ _____
- ○ _____
- ○ _____
- ○ _____
- ○ _____
- ○ _____
- ○ _____
- ○ _____
- ○ _____
- ○ _____

Notes

Notes

May

SUNDAY	MONDAY	TUESDAY	WEDNESDAY
01	02	03	0
08 MOTHER'S DAY	09	10	
15	16	17	
22	23	24	2
29	30 MEMORIAL DAY	31	

2022

THURSDAY	FRIDAY	SATURDAY	GOALS
05	06	07	_____
NCO DE MAYO			_____
12	13	14	_____
19	20	21	_____
26	27	28	_____
CENSION OF JESUS			

TO DO LIST

- ○ _____
- ○ _____
- ○ _____
- ○ _____
- ○ _____
- ○ _____
- ○ _____
- ○ _____
- ○ _____
- ○ _____
- ○ _____
- ○ _____
- ○ _____
- ○ _____
- ○ _____
- ○ _____
- ○ _____

Notes

Notes

June

SUNDAY	MONDAY	TUESDAY	WEDNESDAY
			(
05 PENTECOST	06	07	(
12	13	14 FLAG DAY	1
19 FATHER'S DAY	20	21	2
26	27	28	2

2022

THURSDAY	FRIDAY	SATURDAY	GOALS
02	03	04	
09	10	11	
16	17	18	TO DO LIST
23	24	25	
30			

GOALS

_____
_____
_____
_____
_____
_____
_____
_____

TO DO LIST

○ _____
○ _____
○ _____
○ _____
○ _____
○ _____
○ _____
○ _____
○ _____
○ _____
○ _____
○ _____
○ _____
○ _____
○ _____
○ _____
○ _____
○ _____

Notes

Notes

July

SUNDAY	MONDAY	TUESDAY	WEDNESDAY
03	04 INDEPENDENCE DAY	05	0
10	11	12	1
17	18	19	2
31 24	25	26	2

2022

THURSDAY	FRIDAY	SATURDAY	GOALS
	01	02	_____ _____ _____ _____ _____
07	08	09	_____ _____ _____
14	15	16	**TO DO LIST**
21	22	23	○ _____ ○ _____ ○ _____ ○ _____ ○ _____ ○ _____ ○ _____ ○ _____
28	29	30	○ _____ ○ _____ ○ _____ ○ _____ ○ _____ ○ _____ ○ _____ ○ _____ ○ _____

Notes

Notes

August

SUNDAY	MONDAY	TUESDAY	WEDNESDAY
	01	02	0
07	08	09	
14	15 ASSUMPTION OF THE BLESSED VIRGIN MARY	16	
21	22	23	2
28	29	30	

THURSDAY	FRIDAY	SATURDAY	GOALS
04	05	06	_____
11	12	13	_____
18	19	20	**TO DO LIST**
25	26	27	

GOALS
_____
_____
_____
_____
_____
_____
_____
_____

TO DO LIST
○ _____
○ _____
○ _____
○ _____
○ _____
○ _____
○ _____
○ _____
○ _____
○ _____
○ _____
○ _____
○ _____
○ _____
○ _____
○ _____
○ _____

Notes

Notes

September

SUNDAY	MONDAY	TUESDAY	WEDNESDAY
04	05 LABOR DAY	06	0
11 GRANDPARENTS DAY	12	13	
18	19	20	
25	26	27	2

2022

THURSDAY	FRIDAY	SATURDAY	GOALS
01	02	03	
08	09	10	
15	16	17	**TO DO LIST**
22	23	24	
29	30		

GOALS

_____
_____
_____
_____
_____
_____
_____
_____

TO DO LIST

- ○ _____
- ○ _____
- ○ _____
- ○ _____
- ○ _____
- ○ _____
- ○ _____
- ○ _____
- ○ _____
- ○ _____
- ○ _____
- ○ _____
- ○ _____
- ○ _____
- ○ _____
- ○ _____
- ○ _____

Notes

Notes

October

SUNDAY	MONDAY	TUESDAY	WEDNESDAY
02	03	04	0
09	10	11	1
	COLUMBUS DAY		
16	17	18	1
23 / 30	24 / 31 HALLOWEEN	25	2

2022

THURSDAY	FRIDAY	SATURDAY	GOALS
		01	
06	07	08	
13	14	15	
20	21	22	
27	28	29	

TO DO LIST

- ○
- ○
- ○
- ○
- ○
- ○
- ○
- ○
- ○
- ○
- ○
- ○
- ○
- ○
- ○
- ○
- ○

Notes

Notes

November

SUNDAY	MONDAY	TUESDAY	WEDNESDAY
		01 ALL SAINTS' DAY	0
06 DAYLIGHT SAVING ENDS	07	08	0
13	14	15	
20	21	22	
27	28	29	3

2022

THURSDAY	FRIDAY	SATURDAY
03	04	05
10	11 VETERANS DAY	12
17	18	19
24 ANKSGIVING DAY	25 BLACK FRIDAY	26

GOALS

TO DO LIST

- ○
- ○
- ○
- ○
- ○
- ○
- ○
- ○
- ○
- ○
- ○
- ○
- ○
- ○
- ○
- ○
- ○

Notes

Notes

December

SUNDAY	MONDAY	TUESDAY	WEDNESDAY
04	05	06	
11	12	13	
18	19	20	
25 CHRISTMAS	26 CHRISTMAS (OBSERVED)	27	2

2022

THURSDAY	FRIDAY	SATURDAY	GOALS
01	02	03	
08	09	10	
IMMACULATE CONCEPTION OF THE BLESSED VIRGIN MARY 15	16	17	
22	23	24	
29	30	31 NEW YEAR'S EVE	

TO DO LIST

- ○ _____
- ○ _____
- ○ _____
- ○ _____
- ○ _____
- ○ _____
- ○ _____
- ○ _____
- ○ _____
- ○ _____
- ○ _____
- ○ _____
- ○ _____
- ○ _____
- ○ _____
- ○ _____
- ○ _____

Notes

Notes

2023
Year at a Glance

January

Sun	Mon	Tue	Wed	Thu	Fri	Sat
01	02	03	04	05	06	07
08	09	10	11	12	13	14
15	16	17	18	19	20	21
22	23	24	25	26	27	28
29	30	31				

February

Sun	Mon	Tue	Wed	Thu	Fri	Sat
			01	02	03	04
05	06	07	08	09	10	11
12	13	14	15	16	17	18
19	20	21	22	23	24	25
26	27	28				

March

Sun	Mon	Tue	Wed	Thu	Fri	Sat
			01	02	03	
05	06	07	08	09	10	
12	13	14	15	16	17	
19	20	21	22	23	24	
26	27	28	29	30	31	

April

Sun	Mon	Tue	Wed	Thu	Fri	Sat
						01
02	03	04	05	06	07	08
09	10	11	12	13	14	15
16	17	18	19	20	21	22
23	24	25	26	27	28	29
30						

May

Sun	Mon	Tue	Wed	Thu	Fri	Sat
	01	02	03	04	05	06
07	08	09	10	11	12	13
14	15	16	17	18	19	20
21	22	23	24	25	26	27
28	29	30	31			

June

Sun	Mon	Tue	Wed	Thu	Fri	Sat
				01	02	
04	05	06	07	08	09	
11	12	13	14	15	16	
18	19	20	21	22	23	
25	26	27	28	29	30	

NOTES :

_____

_____

_____

_____

_____

_____

_____

_____

_____

2023
Year at a Glance

July

Mon	Tue	Wed	Thu	Fri	Sat
					01
03	04	05	06	07	08
10	11	12	13	14	15
17	18	19	20	21	22
24	25	26	27	28	29
31					

August

Sun	Mon	Tue	Wed	Thu	Fri	Sat
		01	02	03	04	05
06	07	08	09	10	11	12
13	14	15	16	17	18	19
20	21	22	23	24	25	26
27	28	29	30	31		

September

Sun	Mon	Tue	Wed	Thu	Fri	Sat
					01	02
03	04	05	06	07	08	09
10	11	12	13	14	15	16
17	18	19	20	21	22	23
24	25	26	27	28	29	30

October

Mon	Tue	Wed	Thu	Fri	Sat
02	03	04	05	06	07
09	10	11	12	13	14
16	17	18	19	20	21
23	24	25	26	27	28
30	31				

November

Sun	Mon	Tue	Wed	Thu	Fri	Sat
			01	02	03	04
05	06	07	08	09	10	11
12	13	14	15	16	17	18
19	20	21	22	23	24	25
26	27	28	29	30		

December

Sun	Mon	Tue	Wed	Thu	Fri	Sat
					01	02
03	04	05	06	07	08	09
10	11	12	13	14	15	16
17	18	19	20	21	22	23
24	25	26	27	28	29	30
31						

TES :

2023

	JANUARY	FEBRUARY	MARCH	APRIL	MAY	JUNE
1						
2						
3						
4						
5						
6						
7						
8						
9						
10						
11						
12						
13						
14						
15						
16						
17						
18						
19						
20						
21						
22						
23						
24						
25						
26						
27						
28						
29						
30						
31						

2023

JULY	AUGUST	SEPTEMBER	OCTOBER	NOVEMBER	DECEMBER

January

SUNDAY	MONDAY	TUESDAY	WEDNESDAY
01 NEW YEAR'S DAY	02	03	0
08	09	10	
15	16 BIRTHDAY OF MARTIN LUTHER KING, JR.	17	
22	23	24	2
29	30	31	

2023

THURSDAY	FRIDAY	SATURDAY	GOALS
05	06	07	
	EPIPHANY		
12	13	14	
19	20	21	**TO DO LIST**
26	27	28	

GOALS

_____
_____
_____
_____
_____
_____
_____
_____

TO DO LIST

○ _____
○ _____
○ _____
○ _____
○ _____
○ _____
○ _____
○ _____
○ _____
○ _____
○ _____
○ _____
○ _____
○ _____
○ _____
○ _____

Notes

Notes

February

SUNDAY	MONDAY	TUESDAY	WEDNESDAY
05 SUPER BOWL SUNDAY	06	07	0
12	13	14 VALENTINE'S DAY	
19	20 WASHINGTON'S BIRTHDAY (PRESIDENTS' DAY)	21	2 ASH WEDNESDAY
26	27	28	

2023

THURSDAY	FRIDAY	SATURDAY
02	03	04
09	10	11
16	17	18
23	24	25

GOALS

_____
_____
_____
_____
_____
_____
_____

TO DO LIST

- ○ _____
- ○ _____
- ○ _____
- ○ _____
- ○ _____
- ○ _____
- ○ _____
- ○ _____
- ○ _____
- ○ _____
- ○ _____
- ○ _____
- ○ _____
- ○ _____
- ○ _____
- ○ _____
- ○ _____

Notes

Notes

March

SUNDAY	MONDAY	TUESDAY	WEDNESDAY
05	06	07	0
12	13	14	
DAYLIGHT SAVING STARTS			
19	20	21	2
26	27	28	2

2023

THURSDAY	FRIDAY	SATURDAY
02	03	04
09	10	11
16	17	18
	SAINT PATRICK'S DAY	
23	24	25
30	31	

GOALS

_____
_____
_____
_____
_____
_____
_____
_____

TO DO LIST

○ _____
○ _____
○ _____
○ _____
○ _____
○ _____
○ _____
○ _____
○ _____
○ _____
○ _____
○ _____
○ _____
○ _____
○ _____
○ _____
○ _____

Notes

Notes

April

SUNDAY	MONDAY	TUESDAY	WEDNESDAY
02	03	04	
PALM SUNDAY			
09	10	11	
EASTER			
16	17	18	
23 / 30	24	25	2

2023

THURSDAY	FRIDAY	SATURDAY	GOALS
		01 APRIL FOOL'S DAY	
06	07	08	
UNDY THURSDAY	GOOD FRIDAY		
13	14	15	
20	21	22 EARTH DAY	
27	28	29	

GOALS

_____
_____
_____
_____
_____
_____
_____
_____

TO DO LIST

- ○ _____
- ○ _____
- ○ _____
- ○ _____
- ○ _____
- ○ _____
- ○ _____
- ○ _____
- ○ _____
- ○ _____
- ○ _____
- ○ _____
- ○ _____
- ○ _____
- ○ _____
- ○ _____
- ○ _____

Notes

Notes

May

SUNDAY	MONDAY	TUESDAY	WEDNESDAY
	01	02	0
07	08	09	
14 MOTHER'S DAY	15	16	
21	22	23	2
28 PENTECOST	29 MEMORIAL DAY	30	3

2023

THURSDAY	FRIDAY	SATURDAY	GOALS
04	05	06	_____
			_____
			_____
			_____
	CINCO DE MAYO		_____
11	12	13	_____
			_____
			_____
			_____

TO DO LIST

THURSDAY	FRIDAY	SATURDAY	
18	19	20	○ _____
			○ _____
			○ _____
			○ _____
			○ _____
CENSION OF JESUS			○ _____
25	26	27	○ _____
			○ _____
			○ _____
			○ _____
			○ _____
			○ _____
			○ _____
			○ _____
			○ _____
			○ _____
			○ _____

Notes

Notes

June

SUNDAY	MONDAY	TUESDAY	WEDNESDAY
04	05	06	
11	12	13 FLAG DAY	
18 FATHER'S DAY	19	20	
25	26	27	

2023

THURSDAY	FRIDAY	SATURDAY	GOALS
01	02	03	
08	09	10	
15	16	17	
22	23	24	
29	30		

GOALS

_____
_____
_____
_____
_____
_____
_____

TO DO LIST

○ _____
○ _____
○ _____
○ _____
○ _____
○ _____
○ _____
○ _____
○ _____
○ _____
○ _____
○ _____
○ _____
○ _____
○ _____
○ _____
○ _____

Notes

Notes

July

SUNDAY	MONDAY	TUESDAY	WEDNESDAY
02	03	04 INDEPENDENCE DAY	0
09	10	11	
16	17	18	
30 23	31 24	25	2

2023

THURSDAY	FRIDAY	SATURDAY	GOALS
		01	
06	07	08	
13	14	15	
20	21	22	
27	28	29	

GOALS

_____
_____
_____
_____
_____
_____
_____
_____

TO DO LIST

- ○ _____
- ○ _____
- ○ _____
- ○ _____
- ○ _____
- ○ _____
- ○ _____
- ○ _____
- ○ _____
- ○ _____
- ○ _____
- ○ _____
- ○ _____
- ○ _____
- ○ _____
- ○ _____

Notes

Notes

August

SUNDAY	MONDAY	TUESDAY	WEDNESDAY
		01	
06	07	08	
13	14	15 ASSUMPTION OF THE BLESSED VIRGIN MARY	
20	21	22	
27	28	29	

2023

THURSDAY	FRIDAY	SATURDAY
03	04	05
10	11	12
17	18	19
24	25	26
31		

GOALS

_____
_____
_____
_____
_____
_____
_____
_____

TO DO LIST

○ _____
○ _____
○ _____
○ _____
○ _____
○ _____
○ _____
○ _____
○ _____
○ _____
○ _____
○ _____
○ _____
○ _____
○ _____
○ _____

Notes

Notes

September

SUNDAY	MONDAY	TUESDAY	WEDNESDAY
03	04 LABOR DAY	05	0
10 GRANDPARENTS DAY	11	12	
17	18	19	2
24	25	26	2

2023

THURSDAY	FRIDAY	SATURDAY	GOALS
	01	02	
07	08	09	
14	15	16	
21	22	23	
28	29	30	

GOALS
_____
_____
_____
_____
_____
_____
_____
_____
_____

TO DO LIST

○ _____
○ _____
○ _____
○ _____
○ _____
○ _____
○ _____
○ _____
○ _____
○ _____
○ _____
○ _____
○ _____
○ _____
○ _____
○ _____
○ _____

Notes

Notes

October

SUNDAY	MONDAY	TUESDAY	WEDNESDAY
01	02	03	
08	09 COLUMBUS DAY	10	
15	16	17	
22	23	24	
29	30	31 HALLOWEEN	

2023

THURSDAY	FRIDAY	SATURDAY
05	06	07
12	13	14
19	20	21
26	27	28

GOALS

_____
_____
_____
_____
_____
_____
_____

TO DO LIST

- ○ _____
- ○ _____
- ○ _____
- ○ _____
- ○ _____
- ○ _____
- ○ _____
- ○ _____
- ○ _____
- ○ _____
- ○ _____
- ○ _____
- ○ _____
- ○ _____
- ○ _____
- ○ _____

Notes

Notes

November

SUNDAY	MONDAY	TUESDAY	WEDNESDAY
			ALL SAINTS' DAY
05 DAYLIGHT SAVING ENDS	06	07	
12	13	14	
19	20	21	
26	27	28	

2023

THURSDAY	FRIDAY	SATURDAY	GOALS
02	03	04	
09	10	11	
	VETERANS DAY (OBSERVED)	VETERANS DAY	
16	17	18	**TO DO LIST**
23	24	25	
THANKSGIVING DAY	BLACK FRIDAY		
30			

Notes

Notes

December

SUNDAY	MONDAY	TUESDAY	WEDNESDAY
03	04	05	
10	11	12	
17	18	19	
24 / 31 NEW YEAR'S EVE	25 CHRISTMAS	26	

2023

THURSDAY	FRIDAY	SATURDAY	GOALS
	01	02	
07	08	09	
	THE IMMACULATE CONCEPTION OF THE BLESSED VIRGIN MARY		
14	15	16	TO DO LIST
21	22	23	
28	29	30	

GOALS

_____
_____
_____
_____
_____
_____
_____
_____

TO DO LIST

- ○ _____
- ○ _____
- ○ _____
- ○ _____
- ○ _____
- ○ _____
- ○ _____
- ○ _____
- ○ _____
- ○ _____
- ○ _____
- ○ _____
- ○ _____
- ○ _____
- ○ _____
- ○ _____
- ○ _____

Notes

Notes

Made in the USA
Monee, IL
05 August 2023